Chagall's World

I am thankful to destiny for having brought me
to the shores of the Mediterranean, in the south of France.
Le Message Biblique, in Nice, is witness to my gratitude.

MARC CHAGALL

Chagall's World

REFLECTIONS FROM THE MEDITERRANEAN

Conversations with André Verdet
Portrait Photographs by Bill Wyman

THE DIAL PRESS
DOUBLEDAY & COMPANY, INC.
GARDEN CITY, NEW YORK
1984

Portrait photographs by Bill Wyman on pages: 4, 11, 18, 22, 23, 25, 30, 31, 34, 35, 38, 42, 44, 45, 51, 55, 60, 61, 66, 110.
Watercolors and original drawings by Marc Chagall on pages: 9, 12, 15, 16, 20, 32, 40, 49, 52, 53, 56, 59, 62, 69, 70, 73, 74, 76, 77, 78, 80, 83, 85, 86, 89, 92, 95, 96, 99, 100, 101, 111, 113, 114, 117, 120.
Photograph on page 104 by Serge Ephraim.
Photographs of artwork by Claude Gaspari, Galerie Maeght Lelong, on pages: 9, 12, 15, 16, 20, 32, 40, 49, 52, 53, 56, 59, 62, 69, 70, 73, 74, 76, 77, 78, 80, 83, 85, 86, 89, 92, 95, 96, 99, 100, 101, 111, 113, 114, 117, 120.

Originally published as *Chagall Méditerranéen*
Copyright © 1983 by Galerie Maeght
Photographs copyright © 1983 by Ripple Publications, Ltd.
Artwork copyright © 1983 by Marc Chagall
Translation copyright © 1984 by Galerie Maeght Lelong, Paris

Library of Congress Cataloging in Publication Data

Verdet, André.
  Chagall's world

  1. Chagall, Marc, 1887–   . I. Wyman, Bill.
II. Title.
N6999.C46V4713   1984   709'.2'4   84-4056
ISBN 0-385-19324-6

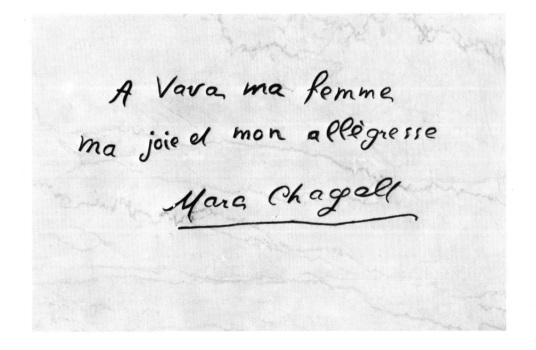

Chagall's World

1948 . . . Back to France . . . After exile in the United States, Marc Chagall was deeply glad to be treading the soil of his adopted country again, but eager nonetheless for peace and quiet, away from city life—not to forget what he had been through, but so that it might help his inner recovery. He found a home at Orgeval, near Saint-Germain. The country atmosphere filled his flower paintings and landscapes. The village steeple is as prominent in these paintings as the steeple of far-off, abandoned Vitebsk had been, just as the steeples of Saint-Jeannet, Vence and Saint-Paul were later to arise in their turn.

While working on *La Nuit d'Orgeval,* the artist thought nostalgically back to the south and Haute Provence, to the old house he had lived in at Gordes, near Apt, for the first few months of the occupation, and, further back still, to the wooded countryside at Peïra Cava in the Alpes Maritimes, where he had several times stayed between 1925 and 1930. Inside him he could hear an insistent call, the call of light, of space made into blue sky. The call was soon to turn into hope.

In 1949, by way of testing the ground before taking the great decision, the artist went to stay first at Saint-Jean-Cap-Ferrat, near his friend Tériade, the publisher, and then at Saint-Jeannet, not far from Vence. He explored the surrounding countryside, and filled the rest of his time doing gouaches and wash drawings. He rented a villa at Vence, and soon afterward finally committed himself to the Mediterranean life by buying La Colline, a white house on a wooded hillside by a valley.

8

Chagall was captivated by nature in the south. Light in the south is not just feeling, but civilization as well. There is the same "inhabited" space that he had known at Gordes. As he steadily took root in this land of the sun, he was attracted to the arts of earth and fire. The ceramics he fashioned and painted in the Madoura workshops at Vallauris are a transposition of his painting into colored sculpture, lightened—just like the paintings—by teeming pigments and the coloring of legend, so that it floats in a dreamlike, weightless space.

A theme began to well up in him, radiating an implacable, calming grace: *Le Message Biblique,* triggered by the spiritual perfection of the votive chapels along the Way of the Cross at Vence. It was like being grabbed by an intoxicating perfume—"a real assault on the emotions," as he was later to say.

To his lasting happiness, the artist had recently married Valentine Brodsky—Vava to their friends—with the grave, unburnished beauty of an icon. With *Le Message Biblique* in mind, Vava now had a big studio built at La Colline. Chagall threw himself unstintingly into *Le Message Biblique.* The effort proved a mental and physical drain, right up to the kind of painful joy he felt on completing it. But he was physically and mentally rejuvenated by *Le Message Biblique,* drawing certainty and comfort from the action of painting it.

The pictures were planned with the same measurements as the chapels. Not a single secular picture was allowed to mar the spiritual unity of *Le Message Biblique,* or to intrude between the initial image and its mental and pictorial realization.

Chagall discovered new depths to his Mediterranean self when he went to Israel and Greece in 1951 and 1954. By the end of his time at Vence, the artist was living intensely, often alone at the bottom of a garden loud with insects and birds in summer, where he sometimes liked to put his canvases under the trees or by banks of flowers, "to see if they stand comparison," to see if they

are indeed a fluidic continuation of nature, and not a betrayal of it.

The works created in the Vence studios grew slowly, not like episodes in a life, but each painting maturing like the fullness of feeling of a whole lifetime.

Paris is the subject of a long series of canvases, which show that the painter had not forgotten what he owed to the capital which had once been his home.

La Danse, Le Cirque (1951), *La Traversée de la Mer Rouge* (1953), *La Nuit de Vence* (1952–56), *Le Concert* (1954–57), *La Femme-Coq* (1956–60)—these are the titles of some of the now famous works created while Chagall was at Vence. During this long spell he finished work on the lithographic sets, *Le Cirque* and *La Bible*. Between 1960 and 1962, the huge mural panel *Ma Vie* was composed for the Maeght Foundation, a kind of all-embracing summing-up of the artist's obsessive themes.

Another mural done at Vence was one commissioned by the Frankfurt Theater, *La Commedia dell'Arte*, a blaring, dazzling orchestration of acrobats, animals, musical instruments and spectators.

Every dawn and every dusk were laden with waking dreams for Chagall—the poetry of unreason or ecstasy, fabulous stories, the whole marvelous, irrational world in which he has created his own myths and pictorial cosmogony. His canvases were still steeped in longing for another world, of innocence and love, but the longing was turning into a fresh, exhilarating transfiguration of colors and shapes.

Sometimes pain and doubt did erupt again, and Chagall painted tragic canvases like *L'Exode* (1952–56) and *La Guerre* (1952–56), which echo *Le Boeuf Ecorché* (1947). But although an underlying disquiet was always there, the way back to peace of mind was to paint flowers and still lifes, with a vision and technique sharpened by his contact with the Côte d'Azur.

Marc Chagall endeavored to be worthy of his good

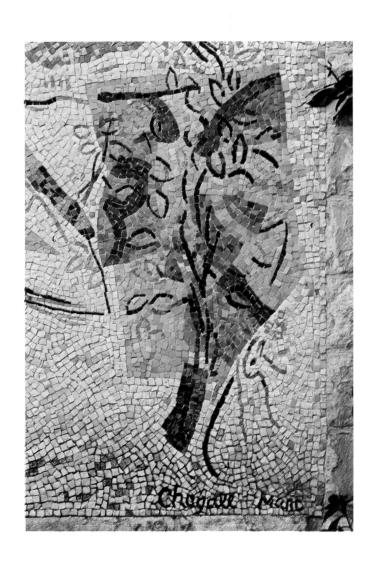

fortune in living by the Mediterranean, a civilizing sea, where the ancient myths are not quite dead but go on haunting a coast still scattered with the ashes of departed gods: the Côte d'Azur, so favorable to discovery of the inner life.

Under the southern sun, a bouquet of flowers or a face or a landscape are not seen in the same way as in Paris or Vitebsk or New York. Under the influence of his surroundings, Chagall's painting seemed imperceptibly to change from within: tiny molecular shifts, tiny new elements showing in the basic chemistry of his pictures. It is not obvious, but has to be detected, like a sort of radiation. It is still not easy to see at first that in some of the Vence paintings, and some of the Saint-Paul ones later on, the drawing takes precedence, with a more ethereal coloring and a feeling more like outer space. Examples are *Le Soleil Jaune* (1958) or *Le Grand Nu à la Corbeille* (1955). The blues in particular—and Chagall's blues are truly regal—take on a sovereign clarity, more like the atmosphere of a brilliant night sky. I am thinking of those blues that are laid like spells onto paintings such as *La Femme-Coq* (1956–60), *Le Repos* (1966) or *Le Poisson Volant* (1966). Chagall is highly sensitive to sounds, his intense, silent attentiveness registering and storing away every image that matters, fragment by fragment. But then one day a complete whole is realized, in harmony with the mental landscape. This mental landscape mirrors not only what the artist has experienced in his present circumstances, but his past experience as well: all transformed and transposed, very slowly and secretly, as through a moulting process in nature.

It would take a decade or two for the Mediterranean to be seen as a definite influence in Chagall's work, inasmuch as each painting needs to mature over time before its intellectual, emotional and plastic essence is finally revealed.

1966. Chagall and Vava have left Vence for Saint-Paul, where they now live, in a sunny spot amidst the restful, salubrious woods of the Bois des Gardettes. Built of local stone, the house was specially designed for work, relaxation and the enjoyment of light.

There are not many flowers in the garden, but plenty in the vases in the big living room. Scattered on the lawn in front of the house are the olive trees Chagall has always loved and wanted around him. On a corner wall is the mosaic *Le Grand Soleil,* a gift from the artist to his wife.

Despite the floods of tourists, medieval Saint-Paul preserves its spellbinding majesty intact, but has not supplanted the picture of his native Vitebsk in Chagall's heart, this little bit of Mediterranean merging in his memory with that far-off corner of Russia. It is in the solar peace of Saint-Paul that the exile, in the evening of his life, has come closest to the land of his childhood, and while giving thanks to his adopted Mediterranean home he is still expressing his gratitude to Vitebsk for its inspiration. The man breathes out a hymn of love, but Blaise Cendrars long ago guessed his hidden pain:

> He takes a church and paints with a church.
> He takes a cow and paints with a cow.
> With a sardine
> With heads, hands, and knives.
> He is Christ.
> He spent his childhood on the Cross
> He commits a suicide every day.

Day by Day, Life and Art:
Dialogue with Marc Chagall

My paintings have often been laughed at, especially the ones with heads the wrong way up or back to front. These criticisms weren't aimed at the way I rendered shapes. In any case, all manner of barbaric reasons have been given for making distortion, or plastic interpretation, fashionable. I did nothing to avoid these criticisms. Far from it. I smiled—sadly, of course—at my judges' pettiness. But I'd still given my life a meaning. And anyway, the painters around me, from Impressionists to Cubists, always seemed too "realistic" to me, if I can put it that way. Unlike them, I've always been most tempted by the supposedly illogical, invisible side of form and mind, without which external truth isn't complete for me. This doesn't mean that I turn to fantasy. Deliberately, consciously fantastic art is alien to me.

If you're a painter, you can put the head at the bottom and still be a painter.

For me, a picture is a surface covered with representations of things (objects, animals, human shapes) in a particular order, in which logic and illustration have no importance at all. Perhaps there's a mysterious fourth or fifth dimension—perhaps not just for the eye—which intuitively sets up a balance of plastic and psychological contrasts, forcing the onlooker to take in new and unusual ideas.

What gives the object its color isn't in fact what's called "real color" or "conventional color."

Likewise, depth doesn't come from so-called laws of perspective.

And likewise, life is what creates the contrasts without which art would be unimaginable and incomplete.

MARC CHAGALL

21

A.V.—Marc Chagall, they've called you a painter of the unreal and a painter of the surreal and a painter of the supernatural. These epithets are all close enough to each other to place your work in that beautiful world of waking dream which is typically yours, a world of perpetual creation which often touches on the marvelous, or even the fantastic.

Now, I think you said one day to Aimé Maeght that your painting isn't realist, but that its roots are deep in the concrete world. And that what you want is for every bit of the canvas or paper you're painting on to be allusive, to refer to *something else:* "When I paint an angel's wings, they're flames as well, and thoughts or desires." Those are your words. Does this mean that in your painting the visible is instantly transposed into *sublimated vision,* so that what you mean by concrete is indeed metamorphosis, with all the elements of the visible unfolding and striking root in an imaginary space, where they take on the quality of poetic symbols, *active* signs with multiple spiritual counterparts?

M.C.—If that's what you think, why not? Anything is possible. Poets have their own way of interpreting things. But if they see fantasy in my painting, it's still not a whimsical fantasy. I never forget the land where I was born. Theories can wait till after the work's finished.

A.V.—When you're working, how is the link set up between poetry and painting, or alternatively, painting and poetry? Is it deliberate, or do you do it intuitively, as you go along, as the controlled magic which you've created slowly grows?

M.C.—Possibly. I can't explain. In the paintings, fusing things become effusive feelings.

A.V.—Seeing and living your pictures, one would think that this world of the imaginary is almost the way you breathe, that it's distilled through every pore of the place where you were born and grew up, in a family steeped in an atmosphere of religious ritual, sacred and secular history, and seemingly timeless stories and legends.

M.C.—Just as you like. The artist harbors memories more than most, and more than most he silently lives them out.

22

A.V.—In your pictures, you seem to me to be stepping out of your earliest childhood. You're an old man now, and laden with honors. Yet you've hardly changed; you slowly emerge from deep in that poor Jewish quarter in far-off working-class Vitebsk, your hometown of country craftsmen. You step forward, dragging behind you in music or dream a sledge or a cart full of memories . . . Now you're going through the streets of Paris, under the Eiffel Tower, along the banks of the Seine, journeying to America and Greece, across the sands of Palestine, along the walls of Jerusalem, finally settling on the hills of Vence, and then of Saint-Paul, looking out on ancient ramparts and steeples, old Provençal belfries and houses, and landscapes which very often seem to change and fuse with the Vitebsk of your dreams.

Yes, for me at least, you've hardly changed, Marc Chagall . . . Despite the crimes and massacres perpetrated by mankind all over the world, you still continue to believe in a fundamental seed of purity, a root of essential beauty, a stem of original goodness, synonymous with innocent, playful mischievousness and poetry—in other words, with love.

M.C.—I do my job as it's come down to me from my forebears over millions of years. That's the greatest Academy in my life. My painting may have played no part in my forebears' lives, but their lives and acts have certainly influenced my art. I find it very hard to talk about my painting. There's only one thing that

guides my hand, and that's the urge to paint, and to offer love with my dreams and colors and shapes, and maybe with that something I was born with and don't really understand myself.

A.V.—But there's such heartbreak in some of your pictures, like a kind of fresh but barely visible scar . . . And all the tragic partings you've been through, exiles and farewells—they're there, under the paint, deep inside or just under the skin, like a muffled pulse. The times you've been torn between two places and wanted to fuse them together in a plainchant of celebration. You actually live your pictures emotionally. The difficulty must be to prevent this sensation taking over, and to use it to achieve the painting you want.

M.C.—If the spirit is pure, then the individual is pure in all he does.

A.V.—In your paintings, the drawing, form, color and medium all seem to be the same substance, part of a single chemical operation. You're outstanding in blending things together. You work on your medium as much as any painter I know, feeding it until it flowers with the richest possible variety of color and perfume. I used the word "chemical," but I could just as well have said "alchemical." Which makes me think of a sorcerer Chagall, mixing oils and essences on his palette like the ingredients of an elixir of life. The physical substance on your canvases seems to be self-fertilizing and self-engendering.

M.C.—Drawing, color and medium are inseparable. Human character is a single whole.

A.V.—You hardly ever use pure tones, and you don't much like the brutal contrasts between them. You work on every one. Take white, for example: it's never pure, but always mixed in with another color or colors. I'm tempted to say that your painting is the typification of *color within color*. Indeed, you actually seem to paint the paint. Another thing is that the medium grows nobler as it ages: there's more in the picture ten years after it's been painted.

M.C.—Quite possibly. If the painting ages well while keeping its freshness, that's fine. That's one of the great secrets in painting. There are some pictures you want to sniff like a bouquet.

A.V.—Tell me what part drawing plays in your work. It seems very much to dissolve, and give way to color, which is perhaps predominant. Sometimes, your line reminds me of the drawings of cave dwellers.

You've only rarely—through exhibitions, for example—given us examples of drawing in its own right, graphically autonomous and unconnected with color. You could, of course, quite rightly retort that your copper engravings are striking examples of your drawing, especially the Bible illustrations and the recent ones which so dramatically accompany André Malraux's text on the Spanish civil war, *Et sur la Terre . . .*

M.C.—I don't know what you see separately in life or art. My eye, for example, sees a whole figure, not color as something separate.

A.V.—In 1950, you made your home in Vence. You've hardly left the Côte d'Azur since then. The Chagall of the isbas and the towns and villages of Russia, the nomadic Chagall of Paris and the Eiffel Tower, America and Mexico, or the journeys to Palestine and Greece, has become the settled, Mediterranean Chagall of Vence and Saint-Paul. We've already seen that the Chagalls of very different places interact with one another. It's like an incantation, fusing the inspirations of the various places. Now, while the basic incantation springs both from your native Russia and from the age-old soil of Jewry, it seems to me that, gradually and secretly, since you settled on the Côte d'Azur, your painting has undergone a subtle, fluctuating change. Not in your favorite themes, but in the chromatic lighting—the way the light vibrates and the colors are applied.

Could one say that this light, and consequently the colors soaked in it, now burn with a richer brilliance and are more *sensuous?*

M.C.—A biography of places where I've lived my life. You, as well as anyone else, are free to see changes in the color and light in my pictures. The painter isn't very aware of these changes, if they exist. Perhaps he only sees them much later. When I did the

Bible etchings, I went to Israel and discovered not only the light, but the soil and subject matter as well. Your surroundings work on you. The light and shade are different, and that finds its own way into the colors. But in my pictures, it's never obvious. My whole life and my work are one.

A.V.—I'm not very familiar with the work you did in the United States and Mexico, when you went to America to escape Nazi persecution. You painted a lot of gouaches out there. Was it a fertile period for you, despite the misery of exile?

Your gouaches are perhaps what best show how steeped you are in the Riviera sky. The forms seem freer, the lines more fluid, the colors more luminous. In other words, your gouaches are more limpid, with a more sensual flavor. It's only an impression, but I feel it quite strongly, and . . .

M.C.—An artist's pictures must be "essentially" the same wherever he's living, even if they seem to have changed.

A.V.—Actually, the word "change" is probably not the right one. Perhaps we should say that a picture has "adapted" to a place, while keeping the same deep roots.

M.C.—As you wish; you may be right, but it's something I just don't notice.

A.V.—In the course of my conversations with Georges Braque, he liked to come back to the artists of the early Italian Renaissance, "the purest and most passionate," he used to say, and then he would go on: "After Giotto, Masaccio, Piero della Francesca, art is mostly eloquence—masterly eloquence, I do admit. Their idea of masterliness at any price has warped our thinking for too long . . . The very thought of this painting is boring. Renaissance artists were more worried about representation than about the picture, and composition suffered as a result. When Veronese paints two apples, it's beautiful—very beautiful, if you like—but for me it's pompous and theatrical. Where's the purity, where's the dazzled, creative innocence that makes you dare to try something new?

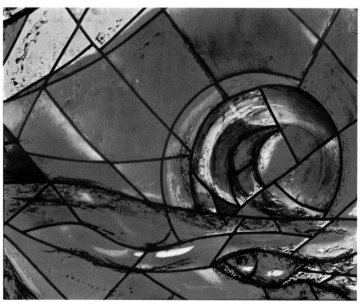

. . . It took centuries to shake off this theatrical attitude. I once wrote that the Renaissance confuses composition with staging (in painting, of course)." Those are Georges Braque's words.

Marc Chagall, I know you like Tintoretto, and the peerless colorist Titian, among others. I have a feeling that Braque's ideas about some of the great Renaissance painters are very different from yours. I might add that Georges Braque's views on the question are curiously like Fernand Léger's.

M.C.—The artist isn't an actor. Think of Piero della Francesca, Giotto, Fra Angelico . . . Or, in France, Rousseau, Seurat, Watteau, Monet, Cézanne . . .

A.V.—On Paolo Uccello, the same Georges Braque said to me: "I suspect Uccello thought about color before what form to give his subject." Do you, Chagall, think about color before form? And since we're talking about Uccello, is he one of your favorites among those famous Renaissance artists—Masaccio, Piero della Francesca, Carpaccio, Bellini, Mantegna?

M.C.—In art, form and color are inseparable. Everything hangs together spontaneously. The Italian painters I like best, of those you mention, are Masaccio, Paolo Uccello and, further back, Giotto.

A.V.—And the Sienese: Simone Martini, Duccio, all pale golden light. You also told me some time ago how satisfying you find the belated gothic of Fra Angelico . . .

I'd like to come back now to something we've already touched on and focus more clearly on the way you work, and, if possible, get a better grasp of the mental and spiritual dominants underlying it.

A long time ago, some critics classed you as a Surrealist, when the movement was just beginning in painting. In my view your painting, then as now, however strange or bewildering or back-to-front or upside-down it may be, however higgledy-piggledy the composition and images, has a popular and religious—or even esoteric—inspiration, combining biblical fervor and pagan, pastoral joy, Judeo-Russian mysticism and Orphism—clearly different from true Western Surrealism.

Your dream visions surely come from an unconscious determined by a sense of the collective and of ethnic symbolism, whereas the dreams and desires of Western Surrealist painters betoken hyper-individualism, and often excessive self-centeredness, captured in a concrete technique which is quite the opposite of yours.

In 1912, at La Ruche, long before he wrote a preface for the Berlin *Der Sturm*, Guillaume Apollinaire looked at your paintings and used the word "supernatural"! . . .

M.C.—He wrote the poem "Rotsoge" for me in 1912. That poem served as a preface to my exhibition at the *Sturm* gallery in 1914.

A.V.—One of Apollinaire's finest poems, which casts light on many of the poems in *Calligrammes*. I know it by heart . . . Including this:

This little painting with a car reminds me of the day
A day made of pieces—purple yellow blue green red
When I was off to the country with a charming chimney
     holding her dog on a lead
I had a tin whistle I wouldn't have swapped
     for a field marshal's baton
There aren't any left I no longer have my little tin whistle
The chimney far away is smoking Russian cigarettes
Her dog is barking at lilacs
And the burned-out night light
On to the dress petals have dropped
Two gold rings near some sandals
Have ignited in the sun
While your hair is like the trolley
Crossing a Europe clothed in little multicolored lights

M.C.—A fine poem! To answer your previous question, I can also give you a text by André Breton, which appeared in *Genèse et Perspectives Artistiques du Surréalisme,* in 1941:

"His lyricism burst right out in 1911. That was when metaphor—with him alone—finally made its triumphant entry into modern painting. Rimbaud had long since prepared the way for the disruption of spatial depth; to complete the process, and at the same time set objects free from the laws of gravity and break down the barriers between things represented and signs, Chagall from the outset gave metaphor plastic support in hypnagogic and eidetic (or aesthesic) imagery, which was not to be described until later, with all the attributes Chagall had given it. There has never been an *oeuvre* more resolutely magic than this, with the wonderful prismatic colors transfiguring and carrying away the pain of modern life—while keeping all the old naïvety of expression for those things in nature which proclaim the pleasure principle: flowers and expressions of love."

A.V.—In the painting *La Mort* (1908), the mood is already disorienting, and there's a man playing a violin on the roof. This image often recurs . . . *L'Enterrement* (1909), *La Noce* and *Le*

Marchand de Bestiaux (1912), *Portrait de l'Artiste aux Sept Doigts* (1912–13), *Au-dessus de Vitebsk* (1914) and *Les Amoureux* (1917), among others. You were already forcing twentieth-century art to accept the amazing freshness of your blossoming new vision, and your wish to give a sense of the union of secular and sacred and raise creatures and things to higher being was already clear. This "upwardness" of feeling only became stronger in your subsequent work . . . Presumably the obsessive recall of your childhood . . . You as a child, a lone watcher on the isba roof, halfway between earth and sky. Juggling with every possible permutation of creatures and things—turning them inside out or back to front or upside down, or combining them in a slightly crazy imaginary world, freed of its weight and already marked by your inventiveness.

M.C.—There was a time when these pictures were laughed at. Some people made fun of my technique. But these paintings are beyond technique: what counts is the love in the painting.

A.V.—Marc Chagall, in some pictures you make us acutely aware—but always poetically—of the tragedy of the Jewish people, their wanderings and sorrows, the criminal oppression inflicted on them, and the heart-rending hope which has guided them down the centuries. The typical Jewish characters are burdened and marked by the misery of people who have been hunted down for millennia. These paintings are more than anecdotal; it's as if we ourselves were suffering the social traumas of a whole race, the tribes of Israel. Did you ever see any pogroms in your youth?

M.C.—Yes . . . My paintings really are my memory.

A.V.—The expression of some of your men and women seems to be postulating another land under another heaven. They're grave and serene in their sorrow, because their suffering is an inner one. Some seem still to be listening to the voices of the prophets. Others, in all their innocence—I'm thinking of the lovers and newlyweds—are lit by such an inner light that they even seem ready to sacrifice the joy they're filled with, at the height of ecstasy. In your work, life seems to surround death and invade it and go on beyond . . . The canvas is like a murmuring wellspring of infinity . . . Atom by atom, the grains of paint are suffused with energy, fluctuating, stubborn energy.

M.C.—The painting is a tissue of flesh, made up of all my thoughts, dreams and experiences . . . A picture stands alone, and its motifs have to ask questions, and provide answers as well.

A.V.—Like all true poets, you are doubtless aware at every second of the never-ending passage of time as something concrete . . . But in your paintings you do capture a little bit of this passing time. It quivers with life in the space you assign to it, like a tiny part of eternity. A few privileged artists can do this, whether painters, sculptors, architects or musicians, and this state of grace is a little victory over death. And no one can say that death will have the last word . . .

M.C.—Thank you!

A.V.—Your canvases very often show ceremonial objects, candelabras, lamps, candles, musical instruments, veils, clocks, books, scrolls and tables of the law, palettes and easels, ladders, etc. . . . In my view, they have quite specific cultural meaning. They're not just put there by accident or for fun. Given ritual value, they surely set up plastic and psychological relations and relationships with other features in the painting—houses and public buildings, people and animals. Similarly with the suns and stars which breathe such magic into your pictures. How do these continuous relations and relationships work in your mind, and . . .

M.C.—They seem illogical and unreal, and yet they exist. They're secret relations, and we do sometimes sense them, but they often escape us.

A.V.—I must say that a lot of your paintings are among the finest examples of *evocative* art that I know. Your work is remarkable in the way it calls to mind popular tales or legends, or religious or pagan myths: they may be alien to us, we may have forgotten them or never have known them, but your painting soon makes them familiar.

M.C.—Everything that makes up our whole age-old existence. I try to make sure that my memory stays active and aware, and doesn't fall asleep.

A.V.—Something worth noting is that your art allows the spectator's eye, and ultimately the spectator himself, ease and freedom of movement within the paintings. This is no doubt because of their atmospheric quality, the soaring, aerial, gravity-defying weightlessness which makes your paintings both very real and rather hard to pin down, like a dream that keeps coming back even while it's fading away. The picture wraps us round with its creatures and objects.

M.C.—The freedom of the spectator's eye in my pictures is the freedom of the brush on the canvas.

A.V.—Most of the animals in your fabulous zoo—or Noah's ark—are made so physically human that we're stirred to the depths of our being. Biological, and sometimes mental, barriers don't seem to exist any more. A kind of salvation through brotherhood.

M.C.—The comparability of people and animals in my paintings isn't accidental, or just an aesthetic or pictorial need.

A.V.—Something like a need for close kinship.

M.C.—I try to create as much as I can with my heart, in the brotherhood of the heart.

A.V.—As for your humans, they're quite often ambiguous. It's certainly easy to tell the sex of most of them—man or woman. But there are sometimes notable hybrids.

A fine Panic sense threads its way through the fable

"of the bull," and mingles with the sense of the sacred. Eros the begetter isn't far from the prophets, the most ancient "composers" of humanity in the Old Testament. The animals are also musicians, instrumentalists on the flute or violin or cello. These are also the characters in your circus, its trapeze artists, actors, ropewalkers, dancers, riders, clowns, angel acrobats and the rest.

I spoke earlier of a far-off Chagall coming toward us through his pictures. Well, do you know, I sometimes imagine you endlessly wandering the countryside with a violin under your chin, like a Russian Orpheus of the east, with the beasts of the air and the earth following on behind. And sometimes the beasts take your place at the front and play in their turn, sometimes floating above the ground or over the rooftops.

M.C.—The poet is free to dream as he likes . . .

A.V.—Christ on the cross sometimes appears in your work, sometimes in the foreground, sometimes at the back. Isn't he the victim of every form of authoritarian oppression, whether religious or political?

And in some of your basically biblical paintings, there are peoples journeying toward some hope, or illusion, or prophetic prediction: aren't they carrying, hidden in the folds of their clothes, or sometimes brandished aloft, the flag of mankind in the throes of expectation? They'll resolve once more to march across deserts, toward a paradise which isn't lost, but is yet to be founded.

Of course the flag does sometimes suddenly appear above the crowd, like an emblem of possible victory . . .

M.C.—They're symbols of misfortune, or of tragedy, or of martyrdom. But symbol doesn't mean symbolism.

A.V.—In your pictures showing Christ, you link His passion with that of the Chosen People. The Old Testament is present in the symbol of the lit candelabra. Presumably this shows the indissoluble union of the Old and the New Testament?

M.C.—You're free to think so.

A.V.—From the very start, right up to the present, your painting is characterized by the poetry of emblem . . . Yet

nothing could be less literary than your pictures. Their thoroughly natural contradictions, whether happy or sad, are smoothed by tranquillity of spirit; the sense of origin and destiny finds justification in a space which you make palpably cosmic . . . Your faith remains as intact as the freshness in these pictures, a consolation.

The animals have eyes filled with tenderness, suffering, credulousness and innocence all together, but nostalgia as well. A hint of joy, but suspended, more like a question, perhaps?

M.C.—People who talk about literature in art don't understand painting or literature. But poetry! I once said: "Show me a single great work where there's no poetry."

A.V.—Did Fauvism—or, later, Cubism—ever tempt you? Did Cubism never impinge on you? Long ago, before the war of 1914–18, when you were working in Paris as a young painter enjoying the friendship of Balise Cendrars and Guillaume Apollinaire, your comment on the Cubists was "let them eat their fill of their square loaves, on their triangular tables."

M.C.—In Cubism I tended to see the formal side, but not the mystical forms which African and ancient peoples have seen. When I arrived in Paris as a young Russian, the Cubist movement was in full swing, but I didn't join it. I often said my pictures were illogical and non-realist, well before Surrealism. It was a kind of realism, if you like, but a psychological realism, and therefore different from that of things or geometrical figures.

A.V.—Guillaume Apollinaire . . . Blaise Cendrars . . . They both used to visit you at La Ruche. Who was closest to you? And what about Max Jacob? In your book, *Ma Vie,* you painted an excellent comic portrait of Apollinaire: "He carried his stomach like a volume of collected works, and his legs waved about like arms."

M.C.—Yes, Cendrars was the closest, and then Apollinaire. I did know Max Jacob, but tended to avoid him. Roger de la Fresnaye was another good friend.

A.V.—Did you sometimes use to meet Picasso, Braque or Juan Gris, or were you, as a young foreign artist, too shy? Like Matisse and Derain, they were already famous, and you were just starting in the "society" of Parisian painters.

M.C.—I met Juan Gris occasionally, and I once visited Matisse.

A.V.—Did you know Malevich and Tatlin well in Russia, and what sort of relations did you have with them?

Malevich took abstraction to heroic lengths. Do you think he contributed in any major way to the break between modern aesthetic thought and the past? The first quarter of the twentieth century couldn't have done without Cézanne's experiments: could it have gone without Malevich the Suprematist, or Tatlin the Constructivist, or Mondrian the Purist?

Reading between the lines of what you say in *Ma Vie* about your time at the School of Fine Arts at Vitebsk, which you founded and where, with Lunacharsky's support, you were appointed principal, it seems that the experience of teaching left a bitter aftertaste, but a feeling of hope as well. Your early excitement eventually gave way to sadness and disillusion, when you left the job.

M.C.—On Lissitsky's advice, I invited Malevich to come and teach at the Academy I founded at Vitebsk. He preached Suprematism to the students, but I never saw anything special or unusual in his color, whether black or white.

A.V.—For you, as for Matisse and Léger—and they made their views clear on this many times—the sacred in art lies beyond any religion. "My only religion is the love of the work I am creating," Matisse said of the chapel at Vence which he'd just finished decorating. As for Fernand Léger, that absolute atheist, he was fond of saying, among other things: "First of all, let me say that the same man—give or take a tenth of an inch or so—created the UN panels, the décor for the CGT Workers' Festival at the Vél' d'Hiv', the décor for Serge Lifar's ballets, *David Triomphant*, the stained glass for the University of Caracas and the mosaics for the church at Assy . . . The same *free* man, with neither preconceived ideas nor split personality." And again: "I just wanted to give *everyone*, believer or unbeliever, a progressive rhythm in color, something useful, acceptable to everyone, simply because happiness and light fill everyone's heart." That's what Fernand Léger wrote and said. I might add that he also did the stained glass for the churches at Audincourt and Courfaivre.

Marc Chagall, you've contributed many monumental windows, mosaics and ceramics to sacred art, and you wrote with

your own hand, on the ceramic *Le Passage de la Mer Rouge* in the church at Assy, "In the name of the freedom of every religion"; but I think that, if asked about your art and the deep, vibrant, mystical spirituality which runs through it, you would give a more qualified answer than Matisse or Léger, because you are actually a *believer,* even if your belief lies beyond any denomination, especially the one you grew up in.

M.C.—An artist is born with or without the sacred in his soul. Masaccio, Giotto, Angelico and others were like that. In this sense, Claude Monet is as religious as Giotto. But artists who paint religious subjects don't always practice sacred art. What I wrote at Le Plateau d'Assy was for all people on earth.

A.V.—Do you sometimes have doubts about the painting you're doing? Do you ever feel so insecure that you think you've not succeeded as an artist?

M.C.—Yes, perhaps, after all kinds of other feelings and, unfortunately, as one starts to get old. Perhaps even a bit before.

A.V.—Since you came to Provence, a lot of your artistic activity has involved stained glass. Your work in this field has, I think, been a major interest for you as sheer research. Has this work given you new ideas for your painting?

M.C.—My first two stained-glass windows were for the baptistry in the church at Le Plateau d'Assy in Savoie. They were commissioned by Father Couturier, a great champion of sacred art, who has been an influence on me.

After meeting Charles Marcq, the master craftsman, I started working in his workshop at Rheims. I did the windows for Metz cathedral, the synagogue in Jerusalem, the chapel at Pocantico Hills, New York, the United Nations Organization in New York, the windows for Tudeley Church in Britain, Fraumünster church in Zurich, Rheims cathedral, *Le Message Biblique* at Nice, and recently, in Gutenberg's beautiful city of Mainz, where he printed the Bible, the windows for Saint Stephen's church. Oh, I nearly forgot the windows for a church at Chichester, in Britain.

A.V.—An impressive body of work.

M.C.—A stained-glass window has a different fate from a painting. Because of the setting, the eye doesn't look at it in the same way as a collection of paintings. The eye of a man at prayer is simply part of his heart.

I've quoted this before, about stained glass: "When you're twenty, you don't think about matter. You have to be old, or to have suffered." People say: "But Chagall, you're all spirit." And I reply: "You have to be spirit to listen to matter." Every color should encourage prayer . . . I can't pray myself, I just work.

A.V.—I'm pretty sure that human beings, uncultured and cultured alike, are more deeply moved by the sublime riddle of the Creation than by anything else art can offer; it throws you into utter solitude, face to face with yourself. Color and light become one, as transparent as sunlight and night-time together, and as they pour through the glass you have an indescribable feeling of being under a spell, and about to share something of the grandeur of the universe, while at the same time you're gradually forced to acknowledge the awesome intimation of the respect we owe the universe—which made us and may unmake us one day—as manifested through all its numberless, vast or tiny creations. What's your view, Marc Chagall?

M.C.—For me, a stained-glass window is a transparent partition between my heart and the heart of the world.

Stained glass has to be serious and passionate, it's something elevating and exhilarating. It has to live through the perception of light.

To read the Bible is to perceive a certain light, and the window has to make this obvious through its simplicity and grace.

A.V.—Stained glass is a stimulus to the inner life, while at the same time it widens the scope of sheer dream, sacred or secular. Life withdrawn into life, and gradually overflowing the borders.

M.C.—Yes.

A.V.—When a picture seems to be finished, and ready to be signed—even if you put off the moment of signing—does having finished it satisfy you? Or are you still uneasy about it, do you still consciously or unconsciously expect to have to add something or take something out later on?

M.C.—Because I often have my doubts, I do hesitate, and tend not to sign until I'm asked to.

A.V.—Let's go back to the substance of your palette, your skillful blending of oils, so rich in content. They say that every painter has his secret. In your case, you give us a feeling of memory, not just through the images alone, but with the actual substance the painting is made of . . .

It's as if the medium itself feels waves of memory going through it . . . An inexplicable something which makes us remember, or rather, puts us into a remembering state . . . in indeterminate time, and without our getting any help from an actual event or its image . . . Matter as memory . . . I've had the same sensation looking at a lot of Jean Fautrier's paintings, and some of Georges Braque's . . . Something like a mental pulsation in matter. What's your view, Marc Chagall?

M.C.—I'd rather leave you to talk about this, and say what you feel. But the more complex the person, the more complex his palette.

A.V.—Could one sum this up, Marc Chagall, by saying that matter is abstraction for you, in that you have to do two things: transcend matter, for it to become a word, look or sound;

and move people by creating something which is surprised to discover its own tragedy and joy, its witchcraft and charms, its doubts and ignorance and certainty—a creation that finds itself believing in its own original mystery and therefore innocence . . . Whence the birth of love.

M.C.—Beautifully put!

A.V.—For nearly thirty years, it's been clear that your work is organized in the form of successive cycles, including especially everything you did for *Le Message Biblique*—the themes unfold and follow on in an organic, spiritual rhythm which could be taken as a counterpart to the cycles of the zodiac, or the wheeling constellations, or the cosmic movements which pervade the Bible . . . Did these cycles appear without your realizing it, or did you deliberately introduce them into your painting?

M.C.—I've always done without theory or method. What you're talking about is simply biblical. I'm not sure myself where some of my ideas can have come from. But they're part of nature, and what seems strange becomes clear. There are still so many things to express in the world.

A.V.—Some of your canvases give a boundless feeling of abundant, teeming life, a life that is very secret and yet familiar at the same time. Scenes in constant movement, joining, matching, slotting into one another, not blindly or haphazardly, but in relation to each other, each keeping its intrinsic visual autonomy . . . Or responding to one another in allusions and echoes, like close or distant counterparts.

M.C.—I try to be life itself. It's life that maneuvers and moves on the canvas, but not with any specific theme.

A.V.—If we look closely at one of your paintings, Marc Chagall, if we examine it and let our eye look beyond what's there and adjust to its depth, we find that the picture is organically built of dozens of others, progressively sparking each other off, scene by scene.

M.C.—It's a picture, and it should be a picture in its entirety. There are hundreds of moments in life which are linked together by art, and turn into paintings I dream about quite outside any kind of realism. It's life itself, and it's got nothing to do with realism or naturalism.

A.V.—You're exhilarated by art, carried away.

M.C.—Loving art is life itself.

A.V.—In your work, disquiet, anguish, tragic suffering, or anything frightening or potentially frightening—all are finally turned into plainchant and peace.

M.C.—I'm afraid I'm too sensitive to too many things inside me and outside me to feel at peace; but this state of mind is essential to art.

A.V.—People, flowers and animals all burn with the simple enthusiasm of ordinary folk, and . . .

M.C.—Yes, I often feel very close to ordinary people, I suppose because I'm from that background myself.

A.V.—Don't you sometimes get the impression—or feeling—that your own pictures are looking at you, questioningly, like another you, who doesn't want to justify himself but is seeking reassurance in mutual agreement?

M.C.—Yes, pictures often look at you, but not reproachfully, if you're pure yourself.

A.V.—Transfigurations and changes or mutations . . . Things or creatures in transformation . . . These people who walk the wrong way round or upside down; or look like ambling animals, or as if they're walking backward; or hover, or fly overhead or away; heads that look unscrewed or twisted back to front . . . All spontaneously invented . . . And sometimes faces and heads like masks . . .

M.C.—It's all invented, of course, but I've experienced it all and, well, it's a picture. It appears spontaneously, and gets structural order from the architecture of the painting. But spontaneity doesn't mean automatism.

A.V.—The circus theme evolved along with the Bible theme, although on a smaller scale. Could you tell me if the secular subject matter correlates with the religious, or do they converge? Was the inspiration for this theme contrapuntal and interdependent with the religious one, or were they twins, closely associated in a greater overall process of spiritual liberation, with the dead weight of earthly thoughts and gestures evaporating up toward a higher world where constraints and contradictions no longer reign?

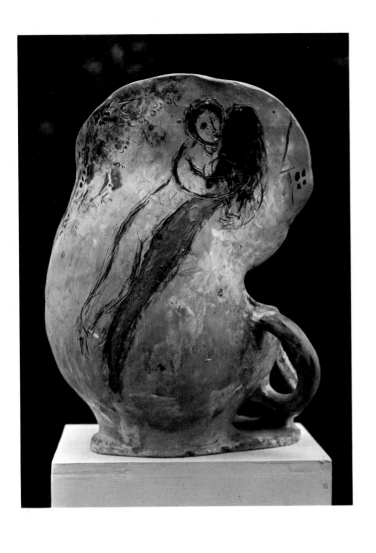
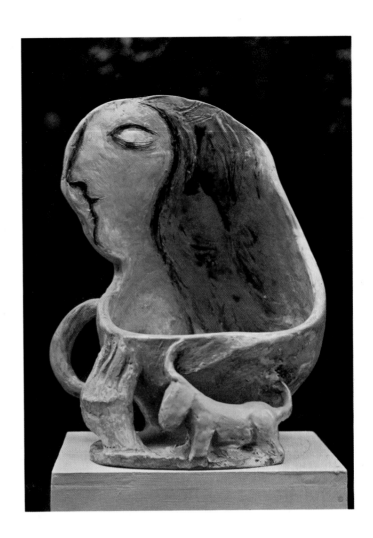

M.C.—I've always seen these clowns and acrobats and dancers as being like characters in some of the religious paintings. They, too, are often tragically human characters. But I don't find it easy to explain the similarity between the two types of paintings.

A.V.—A psychological and plastic convergence.

M.C.—Yes.

A.V.—Having created so many mosaics, involving the choice and application of precious material, has perhaps influenced the full flowering of your palette.

Among contemporary painters, you and Fernand Léger are certainly the ones who have done most mural work, with mosaics, stained glass, tapestries or large-format paintings . . . Are the monumental Chagall and the Chagall of the gouaches, pastels, pencil and ink drawings and oils on paper—the Chagall revealed with such grace and ethereal poetry in the preparatory sketches for *Le Message Biblique*, for example—are these two united in constant harmony in the fluidic application of the medium to construct a work: does the same "spellbound" passion carry over from one form to another? That is, is the wall a successful counterpart to your easel in the *inspired* dynamism of form which is so characteristic of you, the happy radiation of color and shape—the "plastic chemistry" you so value?

M.C.—I've already told you . . . I can judge other people's painting pretty well, but I sometimes find it very hard to talk about my own. I try as much as possible to be myself, all of myself, in any art form, including painting.

A.V.—Before you left France for the United States in 1941, you hadn't done much lithography. You went in much more for engraving, and created three superb albums, Gogol's *Dead Souls*, La Fontaine's *Fables*, where you're full of the sparkle of nature, and *The Bible*. In the United States you did lithographic illustrations for four of the stories from the *Arabian Nights*.

M.C.—I began to get more interested in lithographic work after I came back from the United States and settled in France.

A.V.—Thanks to Tériade, the publisher . . .

M.C.—Thanks to Tériade and his review, *Verve.* I went to the Greek island of Poros to live on the same soil and under the same sky, in the same atmosphere and light as the characters I was going to illustrate. Then I did a set of lithographs for the album *Daphnis et Chloé.*

A.V.—And the theme is raised to the level of myth, as it was in *Dead Souls,* the *Fables* and *The Bible:* the illustration has crystallized into a plastic entity where the essential Chagall is seen, in the creation of universal forms.

I mustn't forget Chagall the ceramist. I remember you working in the Madoura pottery workshops at Vallauris. Biblical motifs above all. It can be an unnerving craft, because fire is the master, and you have to anticipate its whims. Was it settling in Provence that awoke you to ceramic art?

M.C.—I once said: "In Provence, the earth burns your fingers." Before Madoura, I experimented in a pottery at Antibes, a set of plates with motifs from La Fontaine's *Fables*.

A.V.—Starting in 1950, I think. Then there were dishes inlaid with biblical subjects, vases, and tiles painted with Assy's church decoration in mind—all works created in various potteries near Vence. Then finally you came to Madame Ramié's pottery in Madoura.

M.C.—Yes.

A.V.—That was the start of a fertile period: pots, jugs, vases, etc. . . . with a variety of themes. Sparkling, shimmering crockery, yes—but the colors and light are interiorized. These ceramics are completely different from the tawdry brilliance of pure decoration, they're a protest against the flashy, spanking-new, varnished-enamel type of stuff. There's no difference between your painting and your pottery; the one just continues into the other.
Like your paintings, your ceramics shine with an inner light. Most of the motifs are secular, rustic, amorous or dionysiac. Some are as much sculpture as ceramic, and plastically have complete freedom of movement. Your ceramics and pottery avoid the dangers of even the most tempting traditional shapes, and they're both sensuous and civilizing, in the palpable shape they give to all the myths which have for so long haunted your daydreams and your dreams.

M.C.—But they reject decorative stylization. They're a continuation of life.

A.V.—You once said or wrote: "Paintings or ceramics are made with the hands and the heart. Theories can wait till the work's there in front of you—they derive from the work, not the work from the theories." Then, speaking of ancient Chinese or Japanese porcelain or Greek vases, you say that they look stylized, but that "their lines are in fact marvelously free, because these works, too, transcribe the rhythm of life." We ought to agree first on the meaning of "decorative." Henri Matisse accepted its application to his colored paper cutouts, and used to say of Etruscan art that it was decorative but breathed life and movement into matter—actually the opposite of "decorativism."

M.C.—Yes, that's just it.

A.V.—The painter, the mural artist, the printmaker and the theater and ballet designer in Chagall mustn't make us forget Chagall the sculptor. I think it was while you were in Greece in 1952 that you were so moved by the ancient sculptures in the museum at Athens and the sculptures at Olympia. Your first sculptures were done at Father Couturier's request for the baptistry at Assy—small marble bas-reliefs, based on verses from the Book of Psalms. Your statuary brings home your enthusiasm for ancient Greece, early romanesque art and cave art. There's always a pure primitive slumbering in you, who wakes up in spontaneous innocence when the moment of inspiration sounds, like the clear tinkling of a springtime dawn, a cry of lost innocence.

M.C.—Of course, what all this activity means to me is the continuation of my *oeuvre,* something which never stops inspiring me. All the familiar symbols in my work meet up, by osmosis, or instinct, with biblical symbols. For me, it's the never-ending call of continuity.

A.V.—In your house, you spend your time among the flowers arranged in every room by your wife, Vava. Some of these bouquets find their way to your studio . . . All these flowers, from the humblest to the most regal, bring beauty into your day. They speak a language, bringing you a message of hope. They're a summertime symbol for you of that which endures—the unchanging

seasons in the endless succession of centuries. They're an image of renewal and of bliss which we still haven't attained but which is still there within reach of our eyes, nostrils, mouths and hands, but also of our minds. Flowers, Marc Chagall, your flowers? Springtime's offering and invitation—springtime, that you wish might govern the world forever.

M.C.—Perhaps I was poor, and there were no flowers at hand. The first one was given me by Bella. Later on, in France . . . You could wonder for ages about what flowers mean, but for me, they're life itself, in all its happy brilliance. We couldn't do without flowers. Flowers help you forget life's tragedies, but they can also mirror them.

A.V.—Your flowers are fond of metamorphosis, they like to incorporate animals into themselves—take them over, in a way.

M.C.—Yes, people and birds often turn into a bouquet.

A.V.—Yes, they do. Sometimes your flowers are steeped in tragedy and the color of fear—just like your animals, including your favorite, ubiquitous cockerel and donkey.

M.C.—Yes . . . Life and events often take on a tragic look, like some bouquets of flowers.

A.V.—You have written: "One fine day (there's no other kind of day), as my mother was putting the bread in the oven

on her baker's shovel, I went up to her, took her by her flour-covered elbow and said, 'Mother, I'd like to be a painter . . .' "

So that's how it all began . . . . And this memory must have been especially active among the recollections of your parents and of your childhood, which so nourish memory in your pictures.

M.C.—Yes, of course, the parents play a part, and it must be an active one; but so do all one's surroundings.

A.V.—You've painted a portrait of your mother at the oven, dated 1914. Later, you wrote a poem to accompany this image, the proud outline of a peasant woman, as if draped in the gesture of offering bread. Here's an extract:

"Always my heart is heavy—with sleep or a sudden memory, on the anniversary of her death?—when I visit her grave, my mother's grave.

"I seem to see you, Mother.

"You gently come toward me. So slowly that I want to help you. You smile at my smile. Ah, that smile—my smile."

And referring to another painting, *La Femme Enceinte,* of 1912–13, another poem:

If you are my mother, my town
Your son is suffering far away
Hearing nothing of you, nothing from you
In answer to my colors

I can see her, my mother
She waited for me in the doorway
She bequeathed me
A different fate, indistinct

If you are my mother, my town
I am still a stranger
You cannot see the changing cloud
Or the waters of rivers dissolve

My mother on the doorstep used to wait
With her I learned hope
With her breasts she suckled my dreams
Day and night she prayed for me.

Marc Chagall, you've written a lot of poems like this, and no doubt still do. They've been published, and your book, *Ma Vie,* is really one long lyric poem . . . They're swept along in exaltation by the same innocent, playful love, the same fervent love not just for animals and things of nature, but for the cosmos as well. The poet merges into the painter, and painter into poet. They're inseparable, because they thrill with the same rhythms and impalpable coloring, the same floating weightlessness, and the same fluidity in movement and medium . . . Seriousness, humor and downright comedy live happily together in your poems.

M.C.—The paintings and gouaches are also poems. Music and poems in words are also paintings. For example: Shakespeare, Homer, the Bible, Mozart, Schubert, Rousseau, Gauguin, Monet and others.

A.V.—You've become famous all over the world. Your art has been "recognized" by the best essayists and art critics, as well as by the greatest poets of the age . . . If I named them all, it would make a very long list, beginning with Cendrars and Apollinaire and ending with Eluard, Aragon and Malraux. In addition to that, *Le Message Biblique* on the heights of Cimiez in Nice shows the curiosity, the interest and often the genuine admiration which the general public has for your work. You must be pleased today, after so many years devoted to virtually uninterrupted work . . . And there were years of no little suffering or loneliness or disillusion . . .

M.C.—I am thankful to destiny for having brought me here to the shores of the Mediterranean, in the south of France. *Le Message Biblique* in Nice is witness to my gratitude.

A.V.—Your works are witness, in their diversity, to your faith in man, in animals, in Nature, in the deep life of inner realities beyond appearances; and this faith finds full justification in your art, art conceived as moral salvation or a form of mysticism—I'm not afraid of this word, because for you, Nature is *sacred* in all its creations. Sacred in itself, as if by origin. Yes, I think you can be happy to survey the panorama of your works.

M.C.—I don't know. Honesty and sincerity are important qualities for me, and that's all. And then, it's hard to know how to answer, I have so many doubts.

A.V.—You've written that matter is natural, and the natural religious. That seems to me to relate very closely to something you taught me over twenty years ago, when you were still in Vence and I was preparing my first book on your life and work. Your words have remained deeply imprinted on my memory, because they set up an exemplary relation between Nature and Art— a relation which is really a metamorphic fusion. What were your words? "One ought to look at a painting as one looks at Nature. Set a painting up in Nature, out among the trees and the bushes and flowers. It has to stand the comparison. It mustn't clash. It has to harmonize, it has to be a continuation of Nature. Harmonize, however illogical or invented it may look."

M.C.—Yes. You really remember that?

A.V.—Of course. I tell you again, I can feel those words indelibly imprinted in me, like a self-evident truth that's become a physical part of me . . . The famous fluid that runs through a lot of your paintings, which I suppose must be harnessed by your brush as it radiates out of Nature. The first thrill of the Creation, which will last as long as Nature . . . whether it's the breath of Dionysus, Orpheus or God, or of something else we still don't know about. There's the same fluid in Turner, for example, or Pissarro, or Monet, or late Bonnard.

M.C.—Monet sings, he sings! The chemistry is divine . . . His paint itself is sacred. His color is love. I only really recognized this when I came back from America after the last war. A lot of people could only see the "abstract" side to his painting, especially in *Les Nymphéas*.

A.V.—Some of the things you've said recently about color could apply to him. "Color should be as penetrating as walking on a thick carpet"; or, "If you have chemistry, that's the finest ideology."

M.C.—Yes. He's quite incomparable. You have to approach him very carefully. There just aren't the words to talk about his painting.

A.V.—Something else you said links with this—if I remember it rightly—that the chemistry of genuine color and of the paint should be taken as the yardstick of truth.

M.C.—Cézanne, Rousseau, Gauguin, Matisse are modern examples, and El Greco, Titian, Rembrandt and the primitives, further back.

A.V.—You mention Rousseau . . .

M.C.—Some of his pictures make a whole lot of other painting redundant. He's so pure, it's unbelievable! In a picture with a lamp in it, the black of the lamp knocks you backward. It's a black

you can't forget. It follows you about. Not many people have felt the tragedy in Rousseau's colors. People have laughed at him, but he's the glory of France . . . His purity is heartrending, sometimes.

A.V.— . . . and so very silent and lonely.

M.C.—Gauguin's colors, and Van Gogh's, are also very often sad or tragic.

A.V.—Yes, they're blazing colors, but the flames are those of burning sorrow. Colors bleeding inside.

M.C.—They're true, natural colors, they don't lie. When the blood's sick, the body fades. When a color isn't true, the painting is sick as well.

A.V.—A painter's color is true when he feels it deeply, not just in his mind, but in his body as well. The color's true when it's an integral part of the painter, when it circulates inside him and he circulates in it. Like Cézanne's color.

M.C.—Cézanne, Cézanne, a real revolutionary! That's what they say, but how many people really know it? I must emphasize that Cézanne is a truly *unique* case. He didn't want to cover the whole canvas, because he didn't know exactly where he should stop. He didn't finish the canvas. But that's where his genius was.

A.V.—A kind of reserve; not a lack, but the reserve we owe to the mystery of what has already been created and is going to be created again.

M.C.—It's the same with Kafka, in literature.

A.V.—The comparison surprises me. You mean that what applies to the canvas in one case applies to . . . the blank page where ideas have to be written down in words and sentences, or stories . . .

M.C.—Kafka didn't fill everything up either, but with him it was words. The gaps are invisible, but they exist.

A.V.—So that's where the true Kafka . . .

M.C.—My dear Verdet, the truth . . .

A.V.—Might it not be through this reserve—or perhaps "sense of decency" is better—that Cézanne and Kafka want to convey that there's an unviolated area on the edge of creation which we should perhaps respect, and allow to reveal itself in its own natural way . . .

M.C.—On the threshold of the unknowable, Cézanne prefers leaving a space to producing something arbitrary. When he doesn't cover the whole canvas, it's as if it's because the surface is breathing. Cézanne had great artistic dignity. What a figure!

A.V.—To come back to the later Bonnard: like Matisse, he went on developing even in old age. He gave his best when he came and settled at Le Cannet, a few years before he died.

M.C.—And do you like Seurat as well? When he paints his little dots, even in a small space, it's like drops of living light.

A.V.—He's more "underknown" than not understood.

M.C.—Do you think so? He's a reticent painter. We mustn't forget Courbet, either. Fortunately, God gave chemistry to his realism.

A.V.—In some of his pictures, the paint foreshadows Nicolas de Staël's . . . In his forests, his springs and rivers, you sense the presence of the great god Pan, goat-footed mystery . . .

M.C.—And Marquet and his *grisailles*.

A.V.—Once, when you first arrived in Paris as a young artist from Vitebsk, you were filled with enthusiasm for Vincent Van Gogh. Are you still?

M.C.—I still like him, of course. But he shouldn't make us forget Gauguin, who was alone and lost in Tahiti, a world away from Van Gogh and Paris, and the galleries and *salons*. (What I find most moving in Van Gogh is his Dutch period. *Les Mangeurs de Pommes de Terre*—what a masterpiece that picture is!) He got away from Van Gogh and Paris, to try to be more fully himself.

A.V.—I know—everyone knows—what immense love you have for Rembrandt and his work—Rembrandt, another visionary of painting, another "brother seer," as Paul Eluard beautifully put it.

M.C.—Rembrandt simply reduces you to silence. He defeats you, there's nothing you can say.

A.V.—Because he slowly penetrates into the invisible with his whole being, and lights it up with his lamp of the shadows. Yes, we're gripped by silence, as if on the brink of seeing our own destiny unveiled.
But let's come back to you, Marc Chagall, and your blues, your famous blues. Where did you get them from . . . They're some of the most spellbinding blues in the whole of painting. With their native grace, they're the color of legend and divination. They seem to come from the most distant fables, and yet at the same time they seem to spread out into the space of time to come. Blues of the dark before genesis, prophetic blues . . .

M.C.—In my youth, in Russia, I loved walking in the night. I dreamed and dreamed . . . I looked at the stars. I joined in the life of the moving sky. I felt as if I were living another life, parallel to my life on earth.

A.V.—After this conversation, Chagall, I shall take away with me a curious picture of you, which has several times come to me as I've been writing this book: the young Marc, stargazing up on the roof of the family isba . . . Soon flying weightlessly, like a man on a trapeze, over his hometown of Vitebsk, a tightrope poet of the night, over the mean houses, the churches and farmyards; over the sleeping peasants, craftsmen, workers, rabbis and animals; over lovers still awake; over the streets and cemeteries and the fields round about; over the humble joys and great sorrows of the people . . . A young Marc Chagall of the stars, going to meet his destiny, going to meet life as if to meet an age-old prophecy . . . But where does dream begin and reality end?

But just before leaving, one last question. Some time ago, you were invited to Soviet Russia. Officials, artists and writers seem to have given you a friendly welcome. Do you think that the country of your birth—which you served faithfully and whole-heartedly at Vitebsk in 1918, at the time of the Revolution, as principal of the School of Fine Arts—understands your painting better now than it did? And are pictures signed "Chagall," deemed "gratuitous" not so long ago—although there are some in the Moscow and Leningrad museums—at long last a bit more in evidence, becoming better known to the Russian public?

M.C.—I don't know . . . I just work. I go on loving, I don't expect anything more. I hope.

Chagall
Chagall
In the ladders of light

Blaise Cendrars

Eternity Regained

The real spiritual beginnings of *Le Message Biblique* probably go right back to Marc Chagall's stay in Palestine between February and April 1931. Ambroise Vollard had commissioned some engravings for a *Bible,* but the artist had just illustrated Gogol and La Fontaine and, as he said later, "I couldn't see the *Bible,* I could only dream it." Hence the trip to Palestine. Encountering the Holy Land, soaked in the legendary light of centuries, was a shock of revelation, but also a dazzling confirmation that what he saw under the marvelous Palestine sky was just what was expressed in the dreamlike, spiritual side of his earlier biblical work—a longing for the fabled lost land, carried to the height of spirituality.

What he found in Palestine was history incarnate in geography, and still alive, however ancient—history made present through some of civilization's oldest myths and mythologies.

When he returned to Paris, Chagall dashed off a whole lot of gouaches, now part of *Le Message Biblique* at Nice, and in the same flush of inspiration started doing the engravings for Vollard. Between 1931 and Vollard's death just before the war, he made over sixty plates. Finished in 1956, the *Bible* etchings were taken over and published by Tériade in 1957.

The Bible, when he'd heard it read as a child in his native Vitebsk, had sounded to Marc like a golden echo of some awe-inspiring yet tender music. This had carried on through his adolescence, and the reading became food and poetic nourishment, with the essential savor of a centuries-old enchantment distilled by time—the essence savored in many a Chagall painting.

When the young painter began to make his mark, he found inspiration in the New Testament as well as in the Old. In 1910 he did a painting of the Holy Family and a drawing of the Crucifixion, and a gouache of Cain and Abel in 1911. His growing affection for the Bible is shown by various works, such as *Suzanne au Bain*, three paintings of Calvary (1912 and 1913), and two of the raising of Lazarus (1912 and 1913). Then, for fifteen years or so, he seems to have turned elsewhere for inspiration, until he met Ambroise Vollard in 1930.

Bible themes are taken up again in such dramatic pictures as the emotionally intense *Solitude* (1933), *Ange aux Ailes Rouges* (1936), *Chute de l'Ange* (1937), and many others. Then it was the New Testament's turn to provide mystical inspiration, with a num-

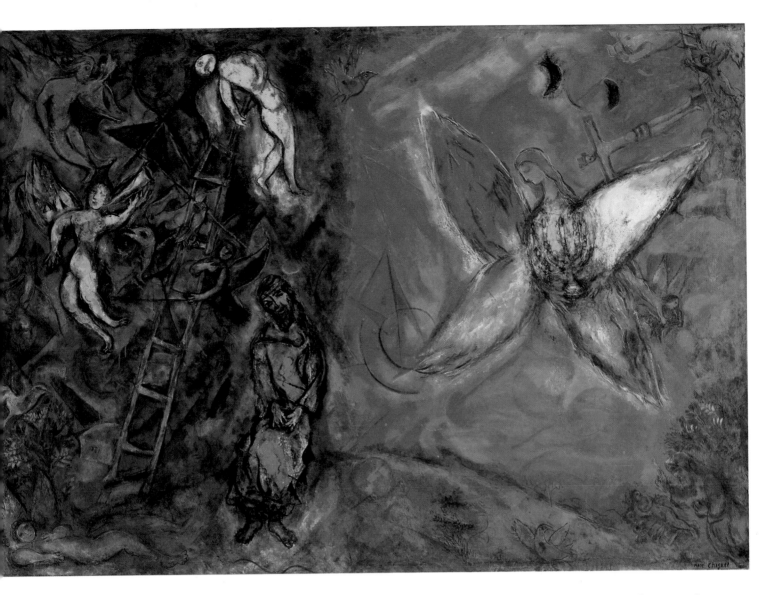

ber of paintings of Christ: *Crucifixion Blanche* (1938); *Le Peintre et le Christ* (1938–40); and *Christ en Jaune, Descente de Croix, Persécution, Christ aux Bougies,* and *Crucifixion Mexicaine,* all painted between 1941 and 1944.

This tragic vein of the crucifixions lasted until 1951, when Chagall returned once more to the Old Testament for inspiration; *Abraham et les Trois Anges* marked the beginning of a rich series of huge canvases: *David, Le Passage de la Mer Rouge, Moïse Recevant les Tables de la Loi, Moïse Brisant les Tables de la Loi.*

1955, Vence. Near Chagall's home there was a Way of the Cross, with one big chapel with attached sacristy, and a set of little votive chapels like stations of the Cross, all disused. Some leading citizens had the idea of getting Chagall to decorate them, and he agreed. He planned to start with the big chapel, the one best suited to decoration because of its size and plan.

Alone in the silent building, the artist spent a long time in contemplation of the blank walls, measuring each one, ponder-

ing his subject matter and blocking out the canvases in his mind. He soon conceived images which then gradually led him along the dazzling path to inspiration . . . a path he had never swerved from since first taking up pencil and brush in an attempt to capture on paper and canvas the world of supernal legend that the Book had told of—a world both wonderful and terrifying, rooted, like a vast sign, in time immemorial.

Fired with enthusiasm for the chapel project, he buried himself in his work. Once he had decided on size and placing, he started painting canvases large enough to fit the walls of the big chapel. He chose the themes of Genesis, Exodus and the Song of Songs. For the end of the apse he painted a *Création de l'Homme*, which was to be flanked on the left and right by *Le Paradis Terrestre*, *Adam et Eve Chassés du Paradis*, *Le Songe de Jacob*, and *La Lutte de Jacob et de l'Ange*. For the south transept, he envisaged *Le Sacrifice d'Isaac* and a *Frappement de Rocher;* for the north transept, *Moïse Recevant les Tables de la Loi* and *L'Arche de Noé;* and for the nave, *Le Buisson Ardent, Abraham Recevant les Trois Anges,* and *L'Alliance du Seigneur avec Noé.*

So from 1955 on Chagall created, with quiet enthusiasm, seventeen canvases. The Vence project fell through, however, and these works can now be seen in Nice, on the Colline de Cimiez. Twelve of them make up the great *Salle de la Genèse et de l'Exode*, the other five gracing the *Salle des Cantiques.*

The seventeen panels in their respective rooms are the same size, and in the same order and position, as the artist had planned to fit the chapel at Vence.

Along with the major collection of studies, gouaches, watercolors and engravings that constitute a perfect introduction to the great main works—pictorial and monumental alike—*Le Message Biblique* truly stands in a *spiritual place;* it is endowed with cosmic symbolism by the demiurgic vision of the painter, filled with a presence and capable of renewing for the modern spectator the images and amazing lyricism of one of the oldest sacred texts of mankind, a text held to be one of the most important and convincing representations of the unceasing, fundamental dialogue, awe-inspiring and comforting by turns, between human beings and God.

Bible stories form part of the history of the Afro-Mediterranean civilizations. Chagall is steeped in them, and he has given us a plastic version of them without parallel in any art. He observes the spirit, indeed the law, of the Scriptures, but his interpretation of the stories makes them something all his own. There is a particular iconography, a pictorial tradition and an anecdotal convention attached to them which he has thrown out, reviving and rejuvenating the stories with fresh force and charm, to appeal to the heart and mind of modern man and make him aware of their ontological meaning and their resounding moral relevance to the complexities of human destiny.

The Word of God in paint. An epic grandeur, sometimes sublime; but in its very mystery it is touched by an aerial fantasy and grace which ensure that it is still familiar. Seriousness seething with touching details. Piercing the heart of tragedy there is always a snatch of dawn—a tenacious and dogged flower. The funny, the odd and the naïve are never far from drama. A starry, peace-bringing idyll shines like an annunciation through the vast, ever-blue night . . . Illogicality seems natural.

The unavoidable confrontation of God and man. Or perhaps even of God and His gods and His men. God and insurgent Nature—for God created Nature, but perhaps it does elude Him sometimes in a leap of freedom.

The stained-glass windows in the music and lecture room, like the mosaic on the patio, are part of the same supernatural atmosphere.

Three windows make up *La Création: Les Eléments,* assigned to the first four days; *Les Espèces,* to the next two; and *Le Repos du Créateur* coming last. The vast, dominant, heavenly ultramarine blue of *Les Eléments* is brilliant with reds, oranges, pinks and greens, constantly changing with the time of day and the light, budding or flowering, glittering or shimmering, floating or deep or withdrawn. At dusk, a sumptuous purple void gradually takes over, with a few last astral shapes still burning up in the shadows of Genesis.

A dynamic window. Contained within abstract shapes launched into space and bathed in creative light, there is a powerful concentration of forces. Forces brought out of chaos, orchestrated, and part of a rhythm already cosmic. Lines of structure clash in wheeling circles and rocketing diagonals, setting up tensions and vectors. It is the dynamism of light, the machinery of the heavens: Planets and Suns.

Cobalt blue is the dominant in *Les Espèces,* the window of the creation of Man, the Beasts and the Plants: Adam and Eve, Serpent, Goat, Birds—all the familiar creatures of Chagall's own teeming fables are there.

The third window, the seventh day—*Le Repos du Créateur*—is full of triumphant angels. Here again, form derives from a powerful, contained dynamism—faceted, prismatic shapes, like jewels set in space, trembling with colors that develop and change as the sun moves round from morning through noon to dusk. There are the same crackling lines of tension as in the other windows.

As usual, Marc Chagall did the work in the Simon workshops at Rheims, in close collaboration with Charles Marcq. He always engaged this master glassworker, because he valued his humanity, creative craftsmanship and intuitive grasp of what Chagall wanted to express in the glass.

The immediate impact of Chagall's windows is of works of art: the light absorbs and dissolves the functional network of lead, as if Charles Marcq's great technique has served the painter's inspiration so well that it has become part of it: a joint effort, but at the end the craftsman's genius has quietly stood aside for a work which could never have emerged without it.

Marc Chagall's job was to paint straight on to glass already bearing the basic colors, a technique known as *grisaille.* The process consists of refining detail and essential shape, the outline being made bolder or less bold, to bring out a particular design. The work demanded dedication and constant vigilance, because the particular functions of a piece in a stained-glass window involve different rules than an oil painting. The artist had to incorporate into the finished work every one of the craftsman's leads. To sensitize the basic medium—in this case the colored glass surface—he also made scratches on the glass (which he called "pecking"), tracing lines all over it like rock carvings or multiform runes. This "pecking" really becomes a series of *signs.* When the sun shines through the window, they are consumed in a triumphant, hallowing apotheosis of color and light. But they still survive in this incessant change as imperceptible particles of swarming life, buried in splendor, like living fossils of space and the air.

On the patio is *Le Prophète Elie,* a monumental mosaic on one of the side walls of the Foundation, over a pond. The water comes up to a line which is actually one of the components of the mosaic. The central figure is Elijah, looming up in his chariot of fire as if in a ship, with the horses as the prow. He is like an apparition, a mass of yellowish greys wrapped around by a kind of astral halo, like the crust of a planet shortly to erupt with Elijah's thundering prophecy.

The signs of human destiny turn clockwise round Elijah and his chariot, in a vivid impression of wheeling stars and constellations, with lightly sketched-in circles making each constellation revolve on itself. The effect is to fix in space the movement and rhythm of passing time, interpreted with a marvelous, ethereal freshness of vision, like images from a children's story. The whole thing sings with the purity and rhythm of a poem of love. The shapes seem to be escaping from a dazzled dream, and to shine iridescent through a fading clear haze, like an impalpable vapor of heaven.

Fertile colors sown in gradations and half-tones. Brilliant germination. Subtle flowering of colors. The shapes, bathed in pools of loving tenderness like perfumes, often have a vigorous, supple line drawn round them, emphasizing the astral rhythms of the composition.

The discreet emotion of sensitive substance. Substance memory-soaked, meaning-laden, in unison with the substance of the windows or oils: an ever-richer chemistry revealed in fluidic matter.

A heap of marvelous bits of stone, marble and glass has imperceptibly been set whirling, and finally arranged on a concrete wall to form a giant palette, where the basic greys seem to me to be what gives the whole composition its iridescence and overall harmony of tone.

The dominant reds at the top right are those of Taurus. Their contrast with the other colors gives movement to the work, drawing the eye up toward the right and toward the blues, and then into the wheeling Zodiac, with Elijah the prophet its guiding master.

Lino Melano, one of the most sensitive master craftsmen in the Ravenna tradition, who had worked for years with leading artists, collaborated with Marc Chagall in the creation of this composition, a perfect example of the painter's success in monumental work.

Now let us return to the body of paintings I was discussing earlier. The really striking, riveting thing is their plastic unity and lyrical kinship. They were all painted at the same pitch of enthusiasm, in the same emotional key, and with images, forms and colors like the rhythms of a symphony from the east, loving and yet wild, as if sprung from an eternal well of fresh-flowing sacred music.

They always include a mass of little details which we must discover in a kind of game—a game of things playing hide-and-seek. Far from distracting our attention, these details strengthen the contribution our eye makes to the picture and the core symbolism of the subject.

Some canvases are noteworthy in that, quite apart from the familiar back-to-fronts and upside-downs of Chagall's vision, he juggles with formal geometry with a fine, provocative freedom. Examples are *Le Paradis, Noé et l'Arc-en-ciel, Le Frappement de Rocher* and *Adam et Eve Chassés du Paradis*, where the vision generated by his deliberately unharmonious distortion of some of the figures is unnervingly strange, especially as they seem at first to collide and

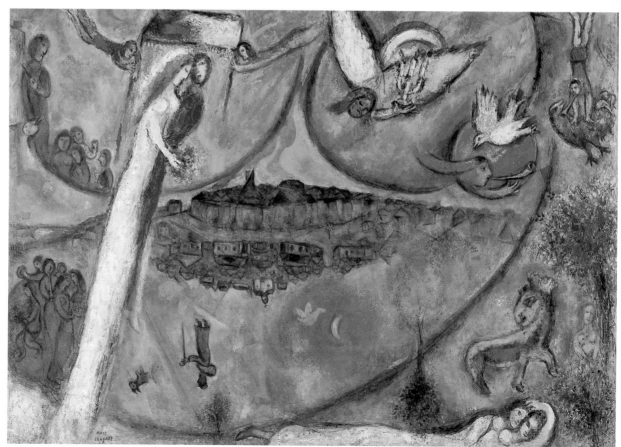

jostle and topple, but then miraculously join in a fragile, trembling balance along invisible vertical or horizontal threads.

Each of the twelve pictures from *La Genèse* and *L'Exode*, then, is pictorially independent, but together they form a wide-screen panorama of the pact which biblical man made with God and kept through a fine, all-embracing frenzy—a pact, but a confrontment as well, naïve and tragic by turns.

The five pictures inspired by the Song of Songs are the plainsong of total love, uninhibited, unrestrained and unforbidden. Heart and soul in love, open to the absolute of loved-and-loving love. And the intrinsic nature of Marc Chagall's painting is such that what might appear to some as an exemplary illustration of a universal religion is actually transfigured and *transcended,* so that the image viewed may resound in the non-dimensional space of a cosmogony of purified soul.

In the enchantment and adorable grace of Solomon's hymn, we take part in the transmutation of physical and carnal pleasures, their fulfillment as spiritual delight.

The unrivaled colorist in Marc Chagall is displayed here in the five successive versions of *Le Cantique des Cantiques* in a glorious, vibrant symphony in red, in infinite flood in its heavenly depths. The surface of each picture seems scented, the perfect counterpart to the *place* of the poem which inspired it, with its offering of mystical flowers and fruits. In some pictures, corbeled balconies of shooting-star orbs give a sense of the wheeling movement of the cosmos.

Les Fiancés and *Les Amants de l'Eternité,* afloat in space, are sailing toward a heaven of supreme bliss. They may be huge and upright, clasping flowery hands, and seem in their embrace to be going off toward the great royal altar, or rocketing starward. The lovers may be riding a seraphic winged horse; or their strange coupling is a metamorphosis stopped halfway, to suggest a fabulous flower-maned creature, doubly half-man and half-beast; or else, accompanied by herald-angel birds, only their faces show, emerging from space as though from sheets on a bed; or else the woman seems at first sight to be the only one in the picture, lying indolently across the canvas, cradled in a leaning tree, sleeping soft and naked with one arm curled round her head . . . But then her lover's face begins to show, in tender ambush, through the leaves.

In these five parts of the Song of Songs, there are figures floating in space which look something like angels or seraphim, tumblers or aerial acrobats. Others—peasants, rabbis, musicians, lone wanderers or anonymous knots of people—walk the earth or are gathered in groups. Domestic animals are also part of the plainsong. And all these creatures, whether motionless or traveling the earth or the sky, *seem to be expecting something to happen.*

In three of the five pictures, the oblong silhouettes of Vence or Vitebsk loom up like ships. Now in *Le Cantique des Cantiques,* the two towns, Russian and Provençal, are joined along the bottom, as if Vence were turning into its inverted echo Vitebsk. This strange refractive effect perfectly illustrates a dreamlike projection typical of Chagall, whereby memory and nostalgia work together to produce a fusion of native land and present home. The twinship thus established is also a spiritual union in both space and time.

This is how Marc Chagall's painting, although tinged with the sorrows and dreams of one who has wandered near and far, is always that of a deeply *rooted* person.

Offering us the chance of solemn heights of joy, *Le Message Biblique* is a place where *exchange* is possible—exchange in meditation, as if our thoughts rose up through all the past layers of history and religion. To those seeking culture and knowledge, this Message will not only yield up part of the infinite and often arcane richness of Scripture; it will also assert that the most meaningful—and meaning-giving—presence is that of the painter inwardly illumined by the Obscure Word of our Origins and Destinies.

As Pierre Provoyeur, curator of the Fondation Chagall at Nice, once said to me: "It is a haven of contemplation, where the tumult of the human spirit is gradually stilled, and turns into daydream and dream, profound and productive."

Cow or donkey cockerel or horse
Even to the skin of a violin
Singing man a single bird
Nimble dancer with his wife

Couple soaked in their springtime

Golden grass and leaden sky
Partitioned by blue flames:
Health and dew:
Iridescent blood and ringing heart

A couple the first reflection

And in underground snow
The opulent vine traces the line
Of a face with lips of moon
Which has never slept at night

PAUL ELUARD, "To Marc Chagall" *(Voir)*

Sacred or Secular Images
for the Mosaics

Marc Chagall's first work in mosaic was *Les Amoureux* (1964–65). It was dedicated to Aimé and Marguerite Maeght, and now adorns the outside wall of the bookshop, on the north side of the Foundation at Saint-Paul-de-Vence, under the trees.

After *Les Amoureux* came *Le Mur des Lamentations*, for a room in the Israeli Parliament, and this was followed by the tender innocence and fresh, rustic calm of *Orphée*, who now sings in the courtyard of the house of Professor Nef, a Washington historian.

January 1967. While still at Vence, Chagall was asked by some of his friends to consider giving a personal touch to the Faculty of Law at Nice, then being built. Maître Trotabas, Dean of the Faculty, approached him on behalf of the student body, Chagall agreed in principle, and they decided on a mosaic. It was apparently after reading *Ulysse ou de l'Intelligence,* by the novelist and poet Gabriel Audisio—who had a perfect grasp of the dazzling mysteries of the Mediterranean mind and its mythologies—that Maître Trotabas suggested the theme of Ulysses, and gave the painter material on various scenes from Homer's legend.

Chagall liked the suggestion, and the thought of getting back to Hellenic antiquity fired his imagination. From then until he left for a trip to the United States, he was on the lookout for any material on Ulysses and his Mediterranean exploits.

When he returned, to his new timber-built house in the Bois des Gardettes at Saint-Paul, he showed Maître Trotabas the sketch for the mosaic. He had chosen the whole of the sug-

gested legend, intending to put all the scenes together into a vast composition exactly following the journey of the *Odyssey*.

Several times a week, Chagall went to make sure that the work was going exactly as he had designed it. Over the fence separating the site from the lecture theaters, the students could glimpse the comings and goings of the precious material. Whenever the painter arrived, they applauded. That was in May and June. Brush in hand, Chagall frequently directed the orchestration of color and shape, to bring a particular shade or line into fuller play. The point of these final touches was to create harmony out of disruption and dissonance, balance out of counterpoint—to ensure the linkage and fit of every detail.

L'Odyssée was finished on 9 August 1968, the fruit of exemplary collaboration with the faithful Italian master craftsman, Lino Melano. Ulysses' was a mind "lit up by intelligence and wisdom," and Chagall carved these lines in response to the general theme of Ulysses' message: "After the Bible Message, I now give Nice that of Ulysses, as a testimony to the manifold wellsprings of the Mediterranean spirit. I hope that, like the sacred splendors of the Bible, the beauties of Homer's poem and the friendship which inspired this mosaic will leave their imprint on the hearts and minds of all the students to whom I dedicate it."

Starting at the top, the scenes go from left to right, beginning (like the *Odyssey*) with *L'Assemblée des Dieux sur l'Olympe*, and showing, in order, *Calypso, Polyphème, Circé, Les Sirènes, Nausicaa, L'Arc, Le Lit Nuptial* and *La Mort d'Ulysse*.

The work as a whole has more physical presence than the *Prophète Elie* mosaic in *Le Message Biblique*, where Elijah seems almost abstract behind the dreamlike pallor filtering shape and tone. The different settings of the works dictate different techniques. *L'Odyssée* is a kind of panoramic view, a large-scale fresco with a more insistent—sometimes violent—rhythm, well suited to the combination of belligerence, lyricism and love in its dynamic hero: the action is punctuated by moments of tenderness and dream which fit in well with the more warlike episodes. *Le Prophète Elie* is mystical, heavenly, aerial, a work conceived in terms of the outdoors. *L'Odyssée* is pagan, terrestrial, oceanic, and conceived in terms of the indoors. The first is full of the ebb and flow of the air. In the second, it is more the backwash of the sea, with the coastal outline suggesting movement; but the mystical Chagall does show through in places, in the hints of seraphim drifting in space. *Le Message Biblique* is an invitation to the visitor to go and see the Ulyssean message, and vice versa. The artist's representation of these scenes is an orphic transmutation, his hand guided by a fervent love and respect for life—the hand, in fact, which led Ulysses on his wedding march through time in the quest for Penelope.

This same trembling fervor spreads its wings in the mosaic *Le Grand Soleil,* dedicated to Vava, at Saint-Paul-de-Vence. A fine sun with spiral leaves fills the center, whirling an embracing couple along with it. Below, the village of Saint-Paul-de-Vence is nestling in the light. A perfume of happiness rises from musicians and trees. A captivating work, like a timeless, pastoral hymn. Here again, the subtle sparkle and freshness of the stones come from the marvelous shading of the greys. This mosaic adorns one of Marc and Vava's garden walls at Saint-Paul-de-Vence.

Still at Saint-Paul-de-Vence, only a few hundred yards from the mosaic at the entrance to the Maeght Foundation, tucked away on a corner wall on the terrace of a private house on a wooded hillside, you might chance on another one, tall and narrow, a secret known to few. There it is, hidden and exquisite, a breathing poem. Happy would be anyone who found it, like a clump of forest flowers among the javelins of sunlight and the tall trees.

This mosaic shows once again the naïve side of Marc Chagall's art. Malraux's comment on the master's paintings applies equally well to his mosaics: "We should not be misled by this naïve wonderment; an art like this is defined not by the fantastic, but by the painterly act, a way of painting which essentially creates poetry. There is no other painter alive who could have painted the Opéra ceiling like Chagall. But just as the painting creates poetry, the poetry creates the painter. Now I certainly respond to Chagall's poetics (which is like Chagall). If all he had done was invent his trembling, innocent, Bible-inspired world, or the ox and the ass of the prophets, he would still be a great artist. But I am worried that that world might be a barrier between his work and the public. Although Chagall is a poet (like Hieronymus Bosch, Piero di Cosimo and many more), he is primarily one of the major colorists of our time."

Among the most recent monumental mosaics, the mural created for the chapel of Sainte Roseline is the one I find most captivating.

Out in the rustic peace of the vines, near Les Arcs en Provence, the chapel stands right up against the old Carthusian convent of La Celle Roubaud. Inside and out, the walls of the medieval abbey (completely restored in 1970 by Marguerite Maeght) whisper the legend of the double miracle wrought by the good and beautiful Roseline de Villeneuve (1263–1329), a gentle nun with eyes of pure wonder. Five years after her death, her still radiantly fresh body was exhumed, to be displayed in a hermetically sealed glass shrine.

Six long centuries later, the saint's body, lying in the nave, is still venerated locally and is the object of a pilgrimage every Trinity Sunday.

Of all the wonders worked by Roseline de Villeneuve's cheerful kindness during her life, the miracles of the roses and the angels early in her youth are the most revealing in Christian legend.

Legends often risk being trivialized by useless or silly frills, and it is no bad thing if they can be stripped of these—for believer and non-believer alike—so that a basic truth about humanity is left free to keep on echoing in the world of miracle, and so that the poetry of legend may fill the hearts of those who accept it with the radiant sense of a higher beauty, lying beyond even belief or non-belief, beyond any dogma, whether religious or secular.

We are led in this direction by the content of Marc Chagall's art.

For in this indoor mosaic, executed by the master craftsman Tharin, the artist is surely trying to restore to us the roses'

freshness and perfume and the taste of the angels' bread—to restore the limpid magic of the medieval romance, and to match it to the kindness and boundless charity of the girl who inspired it.

Roseline is not to be seen in this joyful work: Chagall has "scattered" her everywhere and nowhere. But while absent figuratively, she is present mystically. The tutelary angels around the huge table which they have unexpectedly prepared for the offering of the common meal, really seem to surround her invisible presence with light and to float in a gentle village murmur of simple, frugal dishes, flowers, fruits and branches, bushes, and birds flying off over peaceful cottages . . . You can almost hear the sounds of springtime fledglings in the light of the morning sun. Everything, in this atmosphere of expectancy, seems a promise or a gift.

But suddenly, at the feet of the highest angel, there is a shape, a face glimpsed nestling in a tumble of hair and flowers—surely Roseline de Villeneuve, shyly, reluctantly granting us a glimpse of her young face before retreating into her legendary saint's life even as Marc Chagall's palette sings in her honor: the blues, the greens, the purples and reds and oranges and greys are a consecration of loving tenderness.

It is perhaps in stained glass that the lyrical coloring of Chagall's Mediterranean inspiration found its spiritual and incantatory peak, its plastic and psychological bedrock. Transparent, trembling with light, the lyricism blossoms, as mystically enchanting as any of the famous romanesque or gothic church and cathedral windows. Looking at Chagall's windows, one gets an idea of the special place glass had in the artist's life and work once he had settled in the south of France.

There is no point in analyzing color, form or rhythm, because these are works which simply invade the spectator, like a rising tide of mysterious love from the mists of time, engulfing us in an atmosphere of utter silence and utter contemplation.

Striking the colored glass from outside, the light penetrates the innermost darkness of the church as if from the beginning of the world, when day was still seeking definition in the primeval night.

Stained glass gives a sense of the perpetual penetration of darkness by light, the endless unfolding of color-as-light in the depths of the begetting night. But the windows only become incantations when it is dark: from the outside, seen in full daylight, the glass seems lifeless, the ceremonial plainsong of color and light just a pallid murmur.

Marc Chagall's aim was this: to impart an intense inner life to the object created, by re-embracing the urge and the high ideals of the great stained-glass artists of the past, to make window and building into a harmonious whole.

André Malraux was moved to write: "I cannot understand why stained glass, which lives and dies with the day, was ever abandoned . . . Artists preferred the light. But the stained-glass window, which is brought to life by the morning and snuffed out by the night, brought the Creation home to the worshiper in church . . . Stained glass eventually surrendered to painting by incorporating shade, which killed it. It was six hundred and fifty years before someone found a way of shading off colors in glass: Chagall."

Filtering the art of stained glass through his love, Marc Chagall rediscovered its transparent soul.

The cockerel of fire the first
To denounce the sleep of death
Rips the moon's mask away
A little Parisian cockerel
Hidden in a muffled yard

. . . .

Cockerel of flame! Cockerel-fire!
Burn up our arbitrary dreams
In the ashes of memory

. . . .

YVAN GOLL

Some Thoughts on Animals

For Vava Chagall

A fabulous zoo . . . Noah's ark. Animals made so human that we are stirred to the depths of our being . . . And, sometimes strangely, moved to a feeling of guilt. (Man, that implacable killer of his brother, the beast.)

A deep knowledge of the beasts of stable and farmyard. Of their comings and goings, their familiar movements, their poses, their joys and sorrows and dreaming. The boy Chagall stored it all in his heart. The rustic isba life at Vitebsk has remained imprinted on his memory—not fixed, but floating suspended, with all its smells and perfumes and colors, all the light and shadow of family life, which centered closely on a faith and belief that were proof even against the greatest hardships his family underwent.

An unshakable need to feel the kinship of all the species and creatures in the world. Biological and mental barriers retreat so far that they seem to dissolve.

A kind of blood brotherhood—a salvation.

Some of Chagall's animals even have angel wings. A cockerel takes Christ down from the Cross.

Cockerel, hen, ram, she-goat and he-goat, donkey, horse, mule, dog, cow, pig, birds and fish . . . Surely there is a tiny bit of ourselves in these creatures' "eternal" stare?

But the opposite is also true . . . The human figures so often seem to have in their gaze something of the animal's pathetic eye, something of its immense loneliness and mysterious expectation and handsome pride—and sometimes its fear.

Like human beings, the animals have eyes filled at the same time with tenderness, suffering, credulousness and innocence—but filled with nostalgia as well. Very occasionally, a hint of joy, but almost veiled—more a question, perhaps?

The special place of the cockerel in Chagall's work, right from the start. Tutelary beasts, tutelary cockerels. Here the cockerel protects the lovers under its wing, while the horse watches over them from above. Every creature's eye expands into an obsessive, age-old, ubiquitous, sovereign, sidereal gaze. Elsewhere, like a gentle pageboy, the cockerel leads the bride and groom from the Eiffel Tower to their wedded destiny. Or again, half-cockerel and half-horse, it is hitched to a sledge, whisking a couple and their child up through the air. Or else, in the gloaming, in the village of Vitebsk, it wraps itself protectively round a small child, while the painter at his easel exchanges an adoring kiss with his beloved. And another cockerel that comes to mind has a child riding on its back and playing a pipe.

Gaston Bachelard once aptly compared Leda stroking the swan to the liberties the cockerel takes with some of Chagall's women: "Ah! what would Chagall's cockerels do in life if there were no women? And their beaks—what beaks!"

Cockerel-woman, cockerel-jug, flower-cockerel, tree-cockerel, horse-cockerel, actor-cockerel, musician-cockerel: ambivalence abounds—ambivalence, synthesis or amalgam. And there is

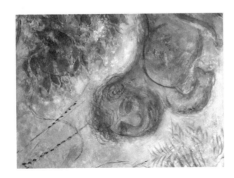

the same manifold play of ambivalence in the sheep, the horse, the cow and the ox . . .

Musician-animals. Instrumentalists, on flute and violin and cello. These are the circus characters, too—trapeze artists, actors, tightrope walkers, dancers, riders, clowns, angel acrobats and the rest.

I see a Noah-Chagall, yes—but an Orpheus-Chagall as well, playing reed pipes or Pan's pipes, violin or cello.

There are some astonishingly, intriguingly ambiguous characters. It is certainly easy to tell the sex of most of them—man or woman—but some are notably hermaphrodite, and there are hybrids in varying degrees of ambiguity. Or you find that the body is human, with an animal's head—or the illogical opposite, which is naturally just as real: an airborne sow in the painting *En Ecoutant le Coq* has a woman's head. Sometimes there is a double face, belonging to two species, man and beast at the same time. In *Songe d'une Nuit d'Eté* (1939), the woman's body is held in a touching embrace by a creature half-beast and half-man.

A religious Marc Chagall, yes, but transcending religion. A legendary Marc Chagall, yes, but beyond legend or fairy tale. A mystical Marc Chagall, yes, but wedded to Chagall the pantheist.

Do the animals, like people, postulate another world under another heaven? I think so. In their heads, there is a world of intuition and instinct, like our world of thought: in their grave, quiet contemplation, there is the melancholy of ages, but they, too, have an inkling of possible consolation.

Doubtless they—Chagall's animals—are amazed that human beings are so cruel. More amazed than some people who love animals for themselves, because their innocence is purer and more spontaneous, less "sullied" by the exercise—almost the technique—of malice which afflicts so many humans.

In the gaze of the creatures in Marc Chagall's bestiary, can I have glimpsed the immense acknowledgment of the beasts—all the beasts, domesticated and wild alike?

·A deep impression was made on the boy Chagall by the sacrificial atmosphere in his grandfather's butchery, where he so often saw beasts slaughtered, their throats slit, and the almost ritual spectacle of bleeding and jointing.

He watched the slaughter in silence. He was not frightened (humans have to eat meat, his grandfather told him), but puzzled and intrigued by these rivers of blood, and already suffering for beast and executioner alike. And full of pity and concern.

He played his schoolboy games among drying skins hanging in his grandfather's house. Every skin brought back a memory . . . a cow he had stroked on the rump before it died . . . a gentle sheep he had kissed on the nose and scratched on the neck as it bleated in fear, before the steel knife sliced into its throat . . .

No doubt the boy Marc sometimes tried to help an animal to die in less fear, tried to see a last look of forgiveness in its eye before it died . . .

Chagall's red: the color of fire and burning coals, the color of spilt blood, thick and warm as if straight from the gaping wound—pure and passionate, the blood of sacrifice.

The ox and the ass . . . Here is what André Malraux writes about them: "Everything he shows comes ultimately from a popular Bible invented by him. With affection. But although the ox and the ass have come down through centuries of Christian painting, they are not in the Gospel. Chagall is the only painter who has had the poetic courage to invent apocryphal prophets in the Old Testament line. Just as the great artists of Assisi knew that the ass would cross its ears to pray, and the ox its horns, so Chagall invents a fauna innocent of the Bible: rabbis on earth, fiancés in the air, wandering clocks . . . A child's world? The ox and the ass would never have survived the centuries if they had just been part of a children's story. And Chagall's figures would not be known all over the Western world if they were just things to wonder at."

Earlier on, Malraux says that whereas Rouault's images are heirs to the world of the Bible, Chagall's are right out on the fringe of the world of Israel.

Poem for Marc Chagall

I have turned for reference to a great, universal book, the Bible. Since childhood, it has filled me with a sight of the destiny of the world, and inspired me in my work. In moments of doubt, its high poetic grandeur and wisdom have brought me peace. The Bible, for me, is like second nature.

I see life's happenings, as well as works of art, through the wisdom of the Bible. A truly great work is shot through with its spirit and harmony. I am not, of course, the only one to think so, particularly today. Since the spirit of the Bible and the world of the Bible have a big place in my inner life, I have tried to express it. The vital thing is to represent those elements of the world which are not visible, not to reproduce whatever we see in nature.

MARC CHAGALL

112

Away from the Edge
and   Towards

The utter omenless dark
With nothing and nothing,
          Untouched,
Placeless, timeless, thingless,
Long before the birth
Of the earliest star, and the first
Planets, the first morning, blue sky,
The golden noon of light,
The primal blue of inaugural night,
The first breath, the first blur
Of the first dream on earth,
The earliest hint of dew.

The first rains and the floods
Over great somber rocks, barely
Cooled and resounding still,
The first wakings of lichen and moss,
The ammonite's first caprice among
Teeming cultures bearing at last
In germ the numberless becoming
Of species and creatures deep
In the primordial rising seas

And seeking definition
In the balance of a skyline.

The first shoot to come through, the forming
Flower's first tryst with
A pubescent sun fresh-sprung
From its matrix of plasma and gas,
The first false starts and Nature's
First displays of triumph.
The first paw raised, the first eye
Light-filled, the first ear
To listen, and the first mouth
On hunger-alert, the first
Genital trance of generation.

For a second I hold my breath
And sense
The first unfolding wing
Take its place in space,
                         And fly in the wind,
Flying flying
              Towards infinity.

The first gestures in their state
Of guileless innocence,
The first experiments of all that
Is born, grows, moves, breathes, dares,
And strives for more
Than to cast a passing shadow.

The primal sap, the primal blood
Of man-to-be in the beast,
The first assessing eye, the first
Protective gesture of love,
The first scent captured,
The first savor tasted,

And finally the first call, the first cry
Of gratitude launched
From the grimmest, furthest depths
Of gorges of darkness
Towards the fire-flares in the sky.

The first brilliant guiding lights
In tunnels of instinct and intuition,
The first laughs and smiles, the first
Embraces and discoveries shared,
The first turmoils of feeling, the surprise,
The first pining dreams and desires,
The first objects selected, the first
Tool fashioned by callow hands, the earliest
Offerings to mystery and the stars,
The first creature reaching upwards
Upright in the urge to flight.

For a second I close my eyes
And see
The first beast's muzzle
Resting on the shoulder of a sitting man.

The first thought triggered,
The first arousal of awareness
To the riddle of death,
The first fires lit
In the heart of the tribal circle,
The first perfect pondered meal,
The first acts of collective affection,
The first hopes, the first doubts,
The first joys and sorrows
Felt and lived through together,

The first memories disturbed
By the stirring memory.

The first struggles, the fights,
The first ordeals, the first judgements,
The first sacrifices of blood spilt
In apocalyptic red
On the altars of hunting and war,
Migration and exile.

For a second I listen to my flowing blood
And feel
The first betrayal.

The first drawing carved, shapes
On the rock of caves
Like a sign to reveal
Ourselves and others,
To exorcise the spells,
The enchantments and witchery
Of bewildering reality,
A roothold in the all-surrounding
Lands of Nature.

The first pure color applied
Like a word at last released,
The first dance to leap
Like sheer dream,
The first music played as if
To escape the heaviness of air.

The first blissful betrothed,
The first wedding consecration,
The first soaring flight of marriage,
The first idol invented,

And the first god set up
Symbolic of belief and
Longing for eternity.

The first preaching seer,
The first thundering prophet,
The first carver of stone
Breathing life into the lifeless,
The first thinker or poet,
The first painter or music-maker
Seeking to transfigure
The haphazards of fate,
The clash of contradiction,
The profits of wisdom,
The temptations of unreason.

Seeking to master
All the variable constituents
Of evil and of good.

     With all this I present you, Marc Chagall.

As I present you with joy or pain,
Peace or suffering.

Anguish or love.

Which with the last face,
With the last tear
Or the last smile,
Will fade
     Away into the spellbound blue
Of the last night.

120

Your blue, Marc Chagall.

The last night of the things and flowers
And creatures of earth.

A world by you made innocent at last, pacified,
Legendary,
         And soaring high.

Beyond your own paintings
And their images and very signs.

                    March–April 1980

Illustrations

Pages 12 and 13. *Le Grand Soleil* (The Great Sun). Mosaic. 1967. 165 × 134 inches. Garden, Colline Saint-Paul.

Page 28. Details of stained-glass windows in the synagogue at Hadassah Hospital, Jerusalem. 1960–61.

Page 29. *La Tribu d'Issacar* (Issacar's Tribe). Stained glass for the synagogue at Hadassah Hospital, Jerusalem. 1960–61. 133 × 99 inches.

Pages 52 and 53. *Les Amoureux et la Bête* (Lovers and Beast). Ceramic. 1957. 12 × 9 inches.

Le Profil (The Profile). Ceramic. 1957. 14 × 11 inches.

La Barque (The Boat). Ceramic. 1957. 13 × 9 inches.

Page 62. *Carnaval Nocturne* (Nighttime Carnival). Oil on canvas. 1979. 51 × 63 inches.

Page 74. *Sarah et Rebecca* (Sarah and Rebecca). Bas-relief, marble. 1972. 52 × 34 inches.

Page 76. *Abraham et les Trois Anges* (Abraham and the Three Angels). Oil on canvas. Undated (1954–67). 75 × 115 inches. National Marc Chagall Biblical Message Museum, Nice.

Page 77. *Le Songe de Jacob* (Jacob's Dream). Oil on canvas. Undated (1954–67). 78 × 112 inches. National Marc Chagall Biblical Message Museum, Nice.

Page 80. *Le Prophète Elie* (The Prophet Elijah). Mosaic. 1970. 282 × 225 inches. National Marc Chagall Message Museum, Nice.

Page 83. *La Création* (The Creation). Stained-glass windows, National Marc Chagall Biblical Message Museum, Nice. On the left: *Les Espèces* (The Species). 184 × 105 inches. On the right: *Les Eléments* (The Elements). 184 × 157 inches.

Page 85. *Noé et l'Arc-en-ciel* (Noah and the Rainbow). Oil on canvas. Undated (1954–67). 81 × 115 inches. National Marc Chagall Biblical Message Museum, Nice.

Page 86. Top: *Adam et Eve Chassés du Paradis* (Adam and Eve Driven Out of Paradise). Oil on canvas. Undated (1954–67). 75 × 112 inches. Bottom: *Le Cantique des Cantiques III* (The Song of Songs III). Oil on canvas. 1960. 59 × 91 inches. National Marc Chagall Biblical Message Museum, Nice.

Page 92. *L'Offrande* (The Offering). Mosaic in the Sainte Roseline Chapel, Les Arcs. 1975. 262 × 225 inches.

Pages 96–97. *Le Message d'Ulysse* (Ulysses' Message). Mosaic, Law Faculty, Nice. 1968. 118 × 433 inches.

Page 100. *La Fête Heureuse* (The Happy Feast). Mosaic. 1971–72. 80 × 40 inches. Private collection. Saint-Paul.

Page 101. *Les Amoureux* (The Lovers). 1964–65. Mosaic, Maeght Foundation, Saint-Paul. 118 × 114 inches.

Page 104. Tapestry for the entrance to the National Marc Chagall Biblical Message Museum, Nice. 1972. 127 × 105 inches.